The Ishtar Gate

The Processional Way
The New Year Festival of Babylon

Gate

Verlag Philipp von Zabern
Mainz

The Ishtar Gate

The Processional Way
The New Year Festival of Babylon

Joachim Marzahn

1992
Staatliche Museen zu Berlin
Vorderasiatisches Museum

The Processional Way and the Ishtar Gate of Babylon

Today, one approaches the Processional Way and the Ishtar Gate from the back. In ancient times, of course, a visitor to the Babylonian capital walked or rode along the Processional Way toward the towering Ishtar Gate. Along the way he could not but admire the magnificent walls lining the Processional Way decorated with roaring lions. To get the best idea of what the ancient visitor might have seen and felt as he approached the city of Babylon, one need only go to the beginning of the Processional Way and retrace one's way toward the Ishtar Gate.

The modern visitor should not be disturbed by the structural division between the galleries housing the Processional Way and the Ishtar Gate. In ancient Babylon, too, the street with its bastions and the forecourt were distinct from the Ishtar Gate (see map of the Royal Palaces of Babylon, endpaper). In the following pages the structures will be discussed separately.

CONTENTS

INTRODUCTION

The Vorderasiatisches Museum of the Staatliche Museen zu Berlin was founded in 1899. The Near Eastern objects in the care of the Egyptian Museum and the objects expected to be added to the collection from the excavations underway in the Near East, were to be combined and exhibited as a separate collection. A temporary display space in the basement of the Bode Museum was used to exhibit the new department of Near Eastern art. In 1929, as the new Pergamon Museum gradually reached completion, the Near Eastern collection moved to its present location in the south wing.

On October 2, 1930 the magnificent Near Eastern architecture halls were opened to the public and by 1936 the installation of the Near Eastern wing was complete.

The reconstructed parts of the Processional Way and the Ishtar Gate of Babylon were immediately not only the heart, but were also the Vorderasiatisches Museum's most popular section. The grandeur of the architectural reconstructions and their brilliantly colored walls and facades offer the museum visitor a unique opportunity to study the accomplishments of an entire epoch of Near Eastern architecture.

The Processional Way and the Ishtar Gate act as the backbone of the Near Eastern Museum. In the adjoining galleries, works of Near Eastern art and archaeology are displayed. The objects in the side galleries are arranged, as nearly as possible, in historical sequence. This booklet is devoted to the Processional Way and the Ishtar Gate, noble testimony of the Babylonian Empire's final flowering. In the closing chapter, the roles played by the Gateway and the Processional Way in the Babylonian New Year Festival are discussed.

THE PROCESSIONAL WAY
OF BABYLON

THE EXCAVATION

As early as 1851, members of a French expedition to Babylon had collected pieces of glazed bricks in the vicinity of the El-Kasr hill ruins that they believed were fragments from a colored frieze. It was not until 1887 that Robert Koldewey and Eduard Sachau examined the fragments of glazed, molded bricks more closely. The men had been sent to the Near East by the Königliche Museen zu Berlin to investigate the ancient ruins of Mesopotamia and select a site for a large scale excavation that might lessen the lead held by Great Britain and France. Under the patronage of leading businessmen and bankers, the Deutsche Orient-Gesellschaft was established on January 24, 1898 to finance the Babylonian excavation and other scientific enterprises. Thanks to its efforts, it was possible for an excavation team to be sent to Babylon in the same year.

Babylon's historical importance, the undisturbed nature of its ancient ruins, and not of lesser importance, the colorful remnants of what appeared to be large edifices, drew attention to the site. On March 26, 1899 the first spade of earth was turned at the ancient city of Babylon.

The excavation was headed by Robert Koldewey, an architect, with the assistance of Walter Andrae, also an architect, and Bruno Meissner, an Assyriologist. The importance of the cooperation between archaeologists and philologists cannot be overemphasized because it was imperative to compare the architectural remains as they came to light with the ancient votive inscriptions.

The excavation was to continue until 1917, and except for Koldewey who only left the site for short holidays, the members of the excavating team changed a number of times. A house built to accommodate the staff, eventually also doubled as a storehouse for the finds which increased with passing years.

Ancient inscriptions indicated that the king's palace lay under the El-Kasr hill, prompting the excavation team to initiate their work at this spot. Specifically, they started on the higher, eastern side of the hill *(fig. 1)* because it provided the best possible vantage point over the ancient ruins. At this stage, no one knew that the Processional Way lay beneath the rubble. A deep trench was dug in the hope of discovering the eastern enclosure wall of the main palace *(see map of the Royal Palaces of Babylon, endpaper)*. In the process, a pair of parallel walls were discovered with rubble completely filling the space between them. The total width of the precinct was about 41 meters.

An ancient inscription stated that the king's palace extended "from Imgur-Ellil to Libilhegalla, the eastern canal, and from the banks of the Euphrates to Aj-ibur-shapu". Initially, one thought this fortification wall was the Imgur-Ellil, one of the city walls, and therefore work was continued westward into the ruins.

Almost all the workers, 200 to 250 strong, were concentrated now in this area. The workers were divided into groups, each headed by a foreman whose job it was to loosen the ground. Three additional workers filled baskets that were then carried away by sixteen additional basketmen. This system of transportation coincided exactly with the millennia old method familiar from ancient inscriptions and representations.

As the work load multiplied, a small railway was set up to simplify the clearing operation. One must keep in mind that in some parts the rubble lay up to 20 meters high over the ruins. The workers cut short trenches five meters apart down the hill to a predetermined point. The process was repeated until virgin ground was reached. As the remains of the ancient walls were unearthed they were, of course, left standing. Usually, several members of the excavation team, also responsible for registration, drawing, photographing and recording the exact find spot of the myriad finds, supervised the work. After the day on the site came to a close, the entry of the finds in the field journal and the daily report in the excavation diary still remained to be completed.

At least in the initial years, the excavation of the Processional Way was a by-product of the excavation of the main palace. Thus, the work in this section was carried on in stages from 1899 to 1902 and again from 1910 to 1914. A systematic exploration of the Processional Way was first made in 1913 when the tops of several hills were "cut off". At the same time, several large trenches were dug diagonally to the Processional Way uncovering the remains of the walls. The results of this part of the excavation are described in greater detail in the following section.

DESCRIPTION

Embraced by monumental walls, the Processional Way ran northward from the Ishtar Gate *(see map of the Royal Palaces of Babylon)*. Its walls also acted as a boundary for the so-called eastern outwork, and on the west, the main palace and the northern palace. In all likelihood, the Processional Way leading to the Ishtar Gate had originally been level with the surrounding area, but, as will be discussed in the chapter on the building of the Processional Way, at some point it was filled to form a ramp ascending

Fig. 1   The beginning of the excavation at the southeastern section of the El-Kasr hill; the picture shows the first excavated part of the second building phase of the Ishtar Gate (for comparison see Fig. 6)

to the Ishtar Gate. Although the reconstructed width of the Processional Way in the museum is only 8 meters, its original width averaged between 20 and 24 meters. The street bed was constructed of mud, sand and rubble that reached a height of twelve to fourteen meters above the original level of the El-Kasr hill in front of the Ishtar Gate. At its beginning, the Processional Way was only about 5,30 meters above the original ground level. At a height of ten and a half meters, an older street surface was found. During its excavation, large sections of the firm, original brick sub-paving set in asphalt were discovered that had served as a foundation for the stone pavement. Little of this original stone pavement was preserved except for an area directly in front of the Ishtar Gate.

The remains of the pavement suggest that like our streets today, the Processional Way was divided into a central traffic lane with pedestrian walkways running along the sides. White limestone slabs (105 cm square and 33 to 35 cm thick) were laid in the central section of the street, and the sides were paved with slabs of red breccia (66 cm square and 20 cm thick), a stone quarried in Northern Syria. The slabs were beveled on the sides and caulked

with asphalt on the underside so that the seams were virtually invisible. The sides of the slabs, naturally not seen by the pedestrians, bore the following building inscription:
"Nebuchadnezzar, King of Babylon,
Son of Nabopolassar, King of Babylon, am I.
The street for the procession
of my great Lord Marduk
I decorated magnificently with stones from the mountains.
Marduk, my Lord, give eternal life!"
The Processional Way was bordered by walls which began at the corner bastions of the Ishtar Gate. With an average thickness of seven meters, and interrupted at intervals by slightly projecting towers, the east wall stretched for 192 meters, and the west wall for 196 meters where a second pair of bastions stood. Walls adjoining this second pair of bastions led northward to a final set of bastions with small corner towers. This magnificent avenue was approximately 250 meters long from the Ishtar Gate to the last bastions in the north. The street ran behind a wide moat that was bridged by a dam with retaining walls. The dam could easily be removed in the event of war, rendering the Processional Way inaccessible. Built on the filled area, the north-eastern bastion was provided with a stairway which probably allowed access to the top of the wall.

The long parallel walls which extended from the first bastion were magnificent. Two long friezes of brilliantly colored glazed bricks bore representations of ferocious lions striding regally down the Processional Way. Not only were the lions differentiated, on the one wall left foot forward and on the other right foot forward, but their coloring varied *(fig. 2)*. There were lions with white fur and yellow manes and lions with yellow fur and red manes *(fig. 3)*. The modern coloration is slightly different because over the centuries the red glaze has turned to green. The lion frieze was set against a background of dark blue and bordered by rows of white rosettes with yellow centers and set between geometric bands of yellow and black and white. Although nothing was discovered in situ, fragments of the lion frieze were found above the foundation walls where they had fallen in more or less their original order and enabled a faithful reconstruction of the frieze.

The findings of the archaeologists made it possible to piece together the overall design. The 180 meter long walls, interrupted at intervals by gates, were originally each decorated with a frieze containing representations of approximately sixty lions. The length of each lion was about two meters. Therefore, two lions decorated each tower wall and two more the corresponding recesses between towers. The partial reconstruction in the Museum, only thirty meters long, is based on these findings. The width of the towers in the museum's reconstruction is in accordance with the archaeologists' finding, six meters wide alternating with a recess of six meters. Resembling the original, the towers project only the width of one brick.

For the ancient Babylonians, lions were not only representations of wild animals, but more important, they were the symbol of the goddess Ishtar who was worshipped in Babylon as the Mistress of the Heaven. In addition, Ishtar was the goddess of love and protectress of the army. Therefore, one can assume that this part of the building lying outside the city was not only meant to demonstrate the size and power of the capital of the Babylonian empire, but even before entering the holy city, the devout Babylonian was reminded of its meaning.

BUILDING TECHNOLOGY

The Ishtar Gate and the Processional Way were erected by the King of Babylon, Nebuchadnezzar II (605–562 B.C.), as part of his comprehensive building program. Unlike his predecessors, Nebuchadnezzar II was not only dedicated to enhancing his capital with impressive buildings, he wanted his monuments to last. This explains why the buildings he constructed were not of the usual sun-dried mud brick, but, for the most part of baked brick. The Babylonian bricks, however, were of a special shape and size; full and half blocks measuring 33 cm square and 33 by 16.5 cm respectively with a height similar to modern bricks. Many of the bricks were stamped with inscriptions which were not visible after the bricks were laid. The bricks were manufactured in the traditional way by pressing clay into wooden forms.

The relief bricks were made in a special way. Each lion is built up of a number of relief bricks that were cast in reusable molds. In this way a sort of production line was set up that made it possible to produce as many identical animals as necessary. The molds were probably cast from an original model that was carefully designed to insure that none of the seams between bricks came at eyes or other places that might be aesthetically disturbing.

To make a molded brick, the first step was to insert the appropriate mold in a wooden brick frame. Then about six or seven lumps of clay were pressed into the relief mold by hand. Often the fingerprints of the ancient artisans can be seen today. Finally, the remaining empty part of the wood frame was filled with clay to complete the brick. After the bricks had dried completely in the sun, they were fired before being glazed. The glazes were made of plant ash and a mineral they called immanakku, probably a sandstone conglomerate with pebbles for the silicates necessary to produce the glaze mass. Then the glaze mass was repeatedly melted, cooled and pulverized. With the addition of mineral colors, precious and semi-precious stones could be imitated. During a second firing, this glaze mass was melted onto the bricks and the bricks were ready to take their place in the long wall friezes. To insure that the right brick was placed at the correct place, the top of each brick was marked with an indication of its position in the overall scheme.

Each lion was made up of forty-six different molded bricks arranged in eleven rows. Mud with a bed of asphalt was used as mortar and in order to increase the overall strength, every fifth row was underlaid with a reed mat instead of mud.

The construction of the gates along the walls is somewhat unusual. Because they were planned with the wall foundations, as the height of the Processional Way was raised several meters, their passageways were simply filled to the necessary height with bricks.

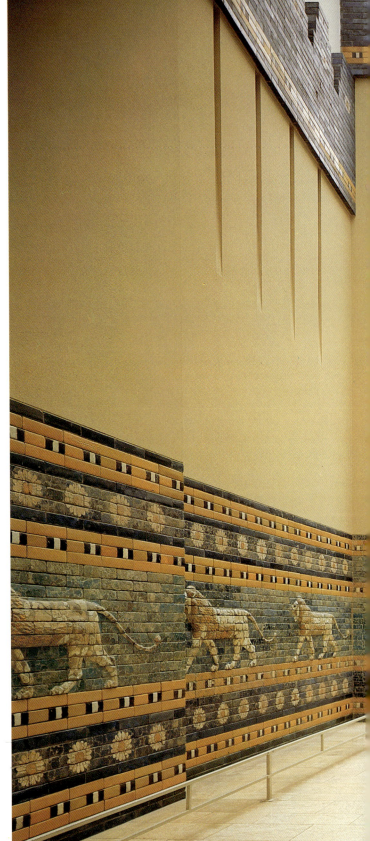

Fig. 2 View of Gallery 8 in the Vorderasiatisches Museum with the reconstructed part of the Processional Way of Babylon

THE HISTORY OF THE BUILDING

Despite what appears to be an extraordinarily comprehensive plan, the buildings were not conceived as a unified structure. Nabopolassar (625–605 B.C.), the first ruler of the Neo-Babylonian (Chaldean) Dynasty undertook a restoration program in Babylon aimed at returning the city to its former glory, that included extending the fortifications and the palace. His son and successor, Nebuchadnezzar II, under whom the empire reached its zenith and final glory, carried on the impressive program begun by his father.

Under his rule, the Babylonian army subjugated the city states of Syria and Palestine. It was part of Nebuchadnezzar's strategy that the architecture of the palaces and sacred buildings of Babylon reflect his might. Not only did he undertake the extensive and grandiose decoration of the major sanctuaries and the old city palace, but he extended the royal palace northward *(see map of the Royal Palaces of Babylon, endpaper)*. The enlargement was carried on in three stages and occurred simultaneously with the raising of the level of the terrain. The eastern wall of the northern palace was extended in the same way. The building sequence can also be followed in the enlargement of the bastions in front of the Ishtar Gate and in the addition of the northern pair of bastions as the level of the Processional Way was raised. The walls lining the Processional Way belong to the third building phase.

Therefore, the parts of the building which were excavated belong to the second building phase and were described by Nebuchadnezzar in the following manner:

"In order that the spear of the Battle not reach Imgur-Ellil, the wall of Babylon, I built the enclosure wall of Babylon, 490 cubits of ground (long), bordering on Nemetti-Ellil, to the outside two massive walls of asphalt and bricks, walls like mountains, and between them I erected a construction of brickwork, on whose crown I built as my royal residence of asphalt and brick a great palace, which I added to the palace of my father."

"In a favorable month, on a suitable day, I firmly established its foundation on the breast of the underground of the earth and I built its head high like a mountain."

Fig. 3 Detail of the Lion Frieze from the wall decoration of the Processional Way from Babylon

"Aj-ibur-shapu, the street of Babylon, I filled up with a high construction of fill for the procession of the great lord, Marduk. With slabs of breccia and mountain stone, I have made Aj-ibur-shapu from Ellu Gate to Ishtar-sakipat-tebisha (Ishtar Gate) suitable for the procession of His Divine Self, with the part that my father built, I connected it (southern part of the Processional Way) and made the way magnificent."

Although we do not know exactly when these monuments were built, it was probably soon after 600 BC at a time when the consolidation of the empire was well along. It should also be mentioned that although the part of the Processional Way nearest the Ishtar Gate was the most spectacular, it was also the shortest. South of the Ishtar Gate the Processional Way ran parallel to the east wall of the southern palace at a distance of twelve meters. It then crossed a moat and curved around the main sanctuary of Etemenanki and ended at the Euphrates bridge *(see map of Babylon, endpaper)*. As the street skirted the south palace it sunk again to the level of the city. Here the street which divided the residential area (Merkes) from the palaces and sanctuaries of the central city was paved with limestone and open at the sides. There were connecting streets at the entrance to the southern palace and at the Etemenanki (ziggurrat of Marduk), the eastern, central gate where a few breccia paving slabs were even found. Thus the street connected the northern city entrance with the entrances to the sanctuary of Marduk, the patron god of Babylon. The name of the entire street was called Aj-ibur-shapu, which means:

"The invisible enemy should not exist!"

THE RECONSTRUCTION

The reconstruction of the Processional Way actually began in Babylon. Every single fragment of the lion frieze that was found was given a field number and marked with its provenance and findspot. Soon after the excavation began, Walter Andrae, a member of the expedition and later director of the Vorderasiatisches Museum, undertook the challenging task of reconstructing a single lion from the fragments. The resulting lion would serve as a model for later work. Much time would pass, however, before the building could be reconstructed. The excavation had to be broken off in 1917 because of the First World War. For seven years the fragments, ordered and carefully packed in hundreds of boxes, remained at the excavation site in Babylon. In 1926, the former Iraqi government permitted the transport of the boxes to Berlin.

Because the fragments of bricks from the Ishtar Gate and the Processional Way were permeated with salt, after their arrival in Berlin they were soaked in vats of water *(fig. 4)*. After the salts had been successfully washed out, the bricks, coated with paraffin, were ready for the assembly which began in 1928 under the surveillance of the sculptor Willy Struck and six to eight assistants. As their work progressed it became clear that the position in which the bricks had been discovered was not necessarily as undisturbed as had been assumed. Occasionally a missing part was found up to 100 meters away. Many bricks had apparently been moved about by brick robbers in the subsequent centuries. The solution was to sort the bricks by types onto large tables, for example, eyes, paws etc. By sorting colors, body parts, right or left foot advanced, it was possible to reconstruct the individual animals with a certain amount of exactitude *(fig. 5)*. It was also a help that during firing hairline cracks had formed between the layer of clay lumps first pressed into the molds and the body of the brick. When the bricks were broken up by brick robbers, they broke along this hairline and with patience and a good eye, it was possible to piece the fragments together. Pieces were reconstructed only when it was certain that they were missing, and then, in such a way that it is clear that they are imitations.

The necessary financial support for the reconstruction of the Ishtar Gate and the Processional Way was taken from the museum building funds — obviously these marvelous examples of Babylonian architecture were structural parts of the museum. The reconstruction of the Processional Way in the central hall of the Vorderasiatisches Museum *(fig. 2)* began in 1929. Closely following the excavation results, the towers and recesses were erected along the walls of the halls and the animal reliefs were set in their

Fig. 4 Glazed brick fragments from the Processional Way and the Ishtar Gate soaking to remove salts, 1928

appropriate places. Today the difference between the original parts and the reconstructed areas is clearly visible. For the most part original bricks were only used for the animals and parts of the accompanying bands of rosettes and geometric design. A complete reconstruction of the lower part of the walls was only attempted on the middle towers. All other parts were reconstructed with modern bricks that were specially manufactured for the purpose. Because little was preserved of the lower parts of the walls,

the reconstruction of the upper parts was problematic. It seemed unlikely that the upper parts of the walls had been completely covered with colored bricks, the preserved fragments were simply not numerous enough. In the Museum's reconstruction the yellowish areas are meant to imitate the mud plastered brick that archaeologists believe completed the walls. The crenelated battlements topping the walls are clad in colored, enameled bricks analogous to the lower frieze although it is not certain if they were

Fig. 5 Working on the identification and rejoining of glazed brick fragments before the reconstruction of the frieze, 1928

so in the original. These crenelations were copied from Babylonian buildings depicted on Assyrian reliefs. It should be noted that the battlements are not provided with a projecting fortification, a type of construction that could only be accomplished with stone or wood, materials not readily available to the Babylonians. Therefore, the cantilever, one brick wide, is in all likelihood correct. The grooves below the battlements were copied from buildings excavated at Assur and correspond to traditional forms of architectural decoration.

Finally, the reconstructed height of the wall, ten to twelve meters, is based on fortification needs in relation to the proportion and the ground plan of the walls, for example, the larger the tower foundation, the higher the tower.

Fig. 6   Remains of one of the gate towers of the Ishtar Gate during the excavation. Clearly visible is the transition from the first colourless building phase (below) to the second building phase in which coloured glazed bricks were used

THE ISHTAR GATE

While in the process of excavating the temple of the goddess Ninmah *(see map of the Royal Palaces, endpaper)*, fragmentary glazed bricks from representations of bulls and snakelike beasts were found in large numbers. From February to November of 1902 excavation work concentrated on the gate building. A limestone block inscribed with a dedicatory inscription found near the gate substantiated Koldewey's theory that the gate in question was the Ishtar Gate. Although the inscription was damaged, from parallels it is possible to reconstruct the inscription as follows:
"(Nebuchadnezzar, King of Babylon, son of) Nabopolassar, (the king of Babylon, am I.) The Gate of Ishtar (I have built) with (blue) glazed bricks for Marduk, (my) Lord."
"Massive bronze bulls (and powerful snake-like beasts ... have

I erected) on its threshold. (With slabs (?) of) limestone (and ...) of stone (have I) the bulls (?) (...?). Marduk, (sublime) Lord, ... eternal life ... grant as a gift."
The name of the Gate is Ishtar-sakipat-tebisha, Ishtar (is) the vanquisher of her enemies.
Early on in the course of the excavation, technically not unlike that of the Processional Way, the first walls were found still clad with up to twenty rows of flat, glazed bricks. Here, the animals of the frieze were only partially preserved and the lower part of a bull was the only beast

Fig. 7   View of the excavation area of the Ishtar Gate after ▷ the exposure of the lower building sections, seen from north. In the left foreground are the remains of the Processional Way's pavement uppermost section

that could be identified. To the surprise of the excavators, however, as they dug deeper a fully preserved snake-like beast and a bull of unglazed brick came to light *(fig. 6)*. These rows of animals were repeated down the gate walls. Not all parts of the Ishtar Gate were uncovered; the southern side was left virtually unexcavated. On the northern side, nine rows of animals were found under the debris with the lowest rows partially under the water table. This meant that the entire foundation of the Gateway was preserved up to a height of 15 to 18 meters. These parts of the building can still be seen in Babylon today *(fig. 7)*.

The decoration on the preserved lower parts of the Gate was quite different from what still remained of the upper portion. Furthermore, quantities of fragmentary glazed and reliefed bricks were found in the vicinity of the Gate which indicated that, like the Processional Way, a number of building stages were involved in its construction. The building phases will be discussed further in the chapter, History of the Building Construction and Reconstruction (pages 24—28). On this part of the building, the development of the facade covering techniques could be particularly well observed.

DESCRIPTION

When Nebuchadnezzar ruled Babylonia, the Ishtar Gate was the northern entrance to his capital, Babylon *(see map of Babylon, endpaper)*. The wall surrounding the old city had five or six gates, including the gate to the Euphrates bridge, each named for a god. The Ishtar Gate was named after the Goddess Ishtar of Akkade whose temple was in the nearby residential area (Merkes). Although the ground plan of the Ishtar Gate was the same as the other gates, thanks to its position at the head of the Processional Way and its proximity to the royal palaces, the Ishtar Gate was more impressive in its decoration.

Two walls of mud brick protected the inner city before which lay a strip of land which was twenty meters wide and supported by a quay wall. A forty meter wide moat offered additional protection from the outside. The strip of land and the moat conformed to the projection of the gates. The opposite bank of the river could be reached by the access road over a narrow dam. Between the dam and the opposite shore, a number of channels at one time permitted the flow of water. The walls of the channels apparently also acted as posts to support bridges which no longer exist. Similar to the construction at the end of the Ishtar

Gate, the dams in front of the other gates could be quickly removed in the event of danger.

We would also expect this typical sort of urban construction in the original version of the Ishtar Gate. It has, however, been lost as the area was mounded up numerous times during its remodeling. Only the ground plan of the Ishtar Gate with its connections to the city walls has been preserved *(fig. 8)*. Following the usual scheme, the smaller gate was situated to the north in the Nemetti-Ellil city wall. Close behind it in the Imgur-Ellil city wall, stood the southern gate. Built to the proportions of the Imgur-Ellil city wall, the southern gate was far larger than its northern counterpart.

Both gates were further protected by a pair of towers at their northern entrance and each had a room which, if we correctly interpret the preserved door casings, had an entrance and exit door. The wings of the doors apparently opened into the rooms in order not to block the passage through the gate. This ground plan is the usual one for double gateway constructions in the ancient Orient.

Two kinds of bricks were used in the construction of the building at Babylon, sun-dried mudbricks and baked bricks. Most common are the sun-dried mudbricks which were the mainstay of Babylonian construction and were here used for areas like the city walls. In contrast, the hard, baked bricks were used to construct the Ishtar Gate and other important buildings.

In front of the Gate was a forecourt that connected it to the Processional Way. In the forecourt, about six meters in front of the western wall which adjoined the north bastion, the remains of a round pedestal with a diameter of 1.40 meters were discovered. The upper part was not preserved and the lower part was walled in with mud brick, probably intended to prevent it from shifting if the ground sunk. Other pedestals were found directly in front of the entrance to the gate at the eastern tower. Although the purpose of these pedestals is unclear, (nothing was found in the vicinity that could have been associated with them), it is thought that they may have served as the bases for the statues Nebuchadnezzar mentions in his inscriptions. The forecourt was formed by the pair of walls connecting the sides of the gate on the north with the pair of northern bastions. The eastern wall, 22 meters long and 9.20 meters wide, had three passageways with stairs leading down to the lower level of the land strip around the city wall.

The western connecting wall, 27.5 meters long and 5 meters wide, only had one passageway through which a seventeen stepped stairway led to the strip of land between the western walls.

In the northwestern side of the gate, a shaft at the level of

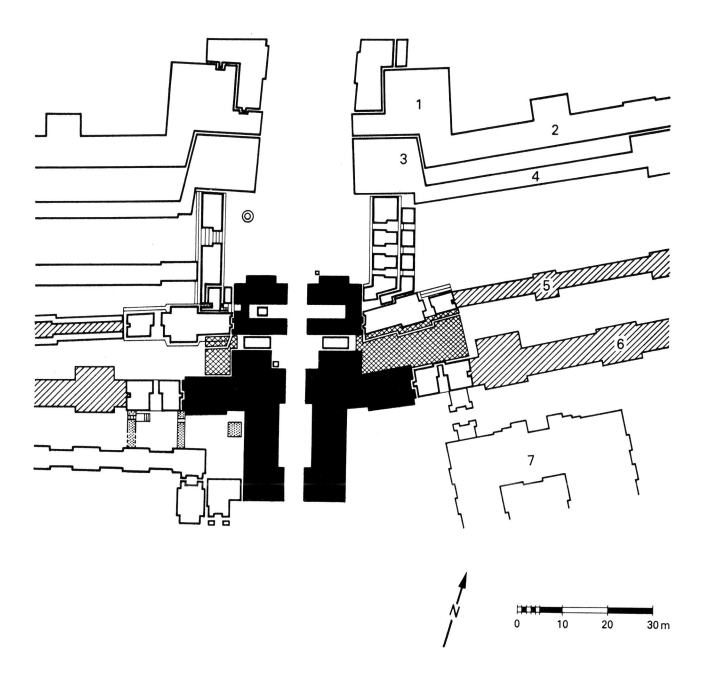

Fig. 8 Ground plan of the Ishtar Gate and its vicinity recovered during the excavation; it shows the second building phase which served as the foundation for the third phase

1 *Younger, northern part of the Bastion opposite the Gate*
2 *Younger Moat Wall of Nebuchadnezzar II*
3 *Older southern part of the Bastion*
4 *Older Moat Wall of Nebuchadnezzar II*

5 *Nemetti-Ellil City Wall*
6 *Imgur-Ellil City Wall*
7 *Temple of Ninmah*

the ground water led to a well with a cistern by means of a narrow winding stairway. The walls of the water chambers had been waterproofed with asphalt which made an ample supply of water available to the guards at all times.

The northern gate with its side towers was 28 meters wide and almost 11 meters deep and projected six meters beyond the city wall. The chamber in the gate was narrow, 3.68 meters, but long, 21.90 meters. The gate passageways, 4.50 meters wide, and the flanking towers (6.20 by 2.02 meters) are reconstructed to original scale in the Vorderasiatisches Museum (fig. 9).

The wings of the doors were never found, but according to ancient inscriptions they were made of cedar with bronze bands. Unfortunately, the door sockets in which the door posts turned were never recovered either. Similar door sockets from Assyria can be seen here in the Museum in Room 3.

The south gate was a good deal larger in relation to the orthers. Its towers alone were 9.05 wide and 4.09 deep. The gate chamber was surrounded by seven meter thick walls and measured 14.90 by 8.05 meters. Here, too, are two door openings lacking doors of the same width as those in the north gate.

Between the walls connecting the two gate buildings was a courtyard which was probably open to the sky. The total passageway through the gate was about 48 meters long.

Side walls connected the gate to both city walls. They, too, had extra passages that could only be entered from the strip of land between the walls. A special technique was used to connect these walls with the gate and the moat wall. Apparently one expected this fill area to sink, so, juxtaposed walls were set into the body of the building with rabbets. Even if the wall shifted to the side, no gap would develop which might weaken the defenses. The same principle was used when the walls of the Processional Way were extended. The area between the side walls at the Ishtar Gate had been filled with brick, and it seems likely that stairs to the top of the wall were located here. Not only is this the most likely place, but no traces were found elsewhere. Unfortunately, the upper part of the wall fill has not been preserved.

THE BUILDING TECHNOLOGY AND DECORATION

The Ishtar Gate is built of hard, kiln baked bricks. The clay used for the bricks was very fine and even. After firing the

bricks were brownish-red. They measured 33 by 33.5 centimeters and had about the same height as our bricks today. Often the square tops of the bricks were stamped with three line, occasionally seven line, inscriptions which would not have been visible when built into the construction. The bricks were made in forms and often after they were removed from the forms, grooves or striations remained on the narrow sides, probably from irregularities in the frames. However, it is also possible that the grooves are a type of marking system. The horizontal seams were filled with liquid asphalt which in the process also seeped into the vertical seams. Unlike the walls of the Processional Way, no strengthening layers of reed mats were found. The horizontal seams between the bricks were unusually narrow, usually only 1 to 6 mm wide. The seams between abutting bricks, however, were so irregular that in some cases the gaps had to be filled with little bits of brick or at least brick grit in asphalt.

The exterior of the building was clad with colored, glazed bricks, or in the case of the animal representations, colored relief bricks. The technique of forming the relief bricks has already been discussed.

The information gained from the excavation shows that two different methods were used to decorate the facade. The lower part of the gate was clad with friezes of bulls and dragons of unglazed, relief bricks. Like the lions on the walls of the Processional Way, these beasts were symbols of a specific deity. The bull was the animal sacred to the weather god, Adad, and the dragon named, Mushhushshu, was the symbol of the city god, Marduk (fig. 10). A partial reconstruction of the animals of the lower building levels can be seen in Gallery 6 at the entrance to Gallery 5 here in the Museum.

The uppermost frieze with the unglazed representations of bulls was smoothed down at some point and covered with white gypsum. Above the unglazed part of the building was part of another frieze with the lower parts of bulls, this time colored and glazed. Instead of relief bricks, flat, glazed bricks were used. A reconstruction of some of these figures can also be seen in Gallery 6. In the process of the excavation, however, numerous fragments of glazed, relief bricks from representations of bulls and dragons were found, so there must have been a third and final building stage above the one preserved.

Fig. 9 The Ishtar Gate in the Vorderasiatisches Museum ▷ (compare cover)

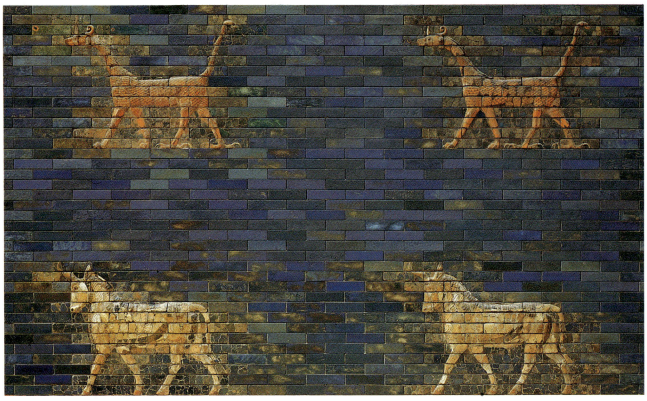

Fig. 10   *Dragon and bull reliefs from the covering of the Ishtar Gate's facade, third building phase*

The History of the Building Construction and its Reconstruction

Like the Processional Way, the construction of the Ishtar Gate was not confined to one building phase. In the previous section we have seen the various methods of building decoration as proof. Although the lion friezes of the Procession Way can only be associated with the final building phase, the magnificent bull and dragon friezes were part of the decoration originally planned for the gate.

The earlier gate, of which nothing remains today, must first have been built at ground level. As the royal palaces were expanded, the area north of the inner city wall changed a number of times. These changes took place in three stages. The first building was clad with unglazed reliefs and probably simply repeated the form of its predecessor. The projection, characteristic of the previous building, as

well as the quay wall, comparable to the form of the other gates, could still be detected.

The following discussion of the Ishtar Gate building phases may be followed on the ground plan *(fig. 8)* and the overall view *(fig. 11)*.

Shortly thereafter, Nebuchadnezzar enlarged the main citadel, filling and raising the Processional Way seven meters. Pavement remains were found at this level which indicate a temporary gateway at a time when part of the gate building was covered in fill. The next well preserved pavement was found several meters higher, at 10.85 meters, and was the pavement for the second building stage. At this height the ground plan of the gate had reached its final form. The pedestals that have already been discussed were part of this second building phase.

In contrast, the new building ended with a pair of projecting bastions north of the gate. With the construction of a pair of connecting walls between the gate and bastions, a forecourt was created. The area at the sides had not been

Fig. 11 Drawing of the complete reconstruction of the Ishtar Gate with sectional view through the deposits of the Processional Way. The deposits for the last building phase are marked in lighter hachure

filled which made it necessary to build stairs in the connecting walls to reach the strip of land between the walls. The part of the unglazed gate facade which now lay above the fill was carefully reworked with scrapers or rasps and now looked very different from the area that was not reworked. The asphalt which had seeped out during the laying of the bricks had not been removed. Because the excavators only found a row of unglazed representations of bulls preserved above the pavement, it is not possible to say whether this unglazed part of the second building phase was continued above.

Directly above this, the building had been changed once again with the addition of at least one row of bulls made of flat, glazed bricks in part still visible in 1902. The remains of flat, glazed bricks found in the vicinity show that at least one row of dragons must have been depicted above the frieze of bulls.

This means that although the gate had been planned with a colored facade at this stage, the uncolored row of animals at pavement level was still visible. To lessen the inconsistency, the bulls were covered in white gypsum, splendidly setting off the colored frieze of animals above.

During the same building phase, a moat wall running to the north and ending in a pair of bastions was constructed. The new bastions adjoined the older ones north of the forecourt in such a way that they seemed like a single structure. The walls embracing the Processional Way, at this point undecorated, ran to the north from the front of this fortification structure.

In all likelihood, the second building phase of the gate with the flat, unglazed animals also was never completed. It was at this point that the king decided to extend his palace to the north beyond the existing city wall. With the city situated to the south, the Euphrates to the west, and the Processional Way to the east which in the king's own words, he did not dare to touch, the only possibility to expand was to build to the north.

The construction of the so-called northern main citadel

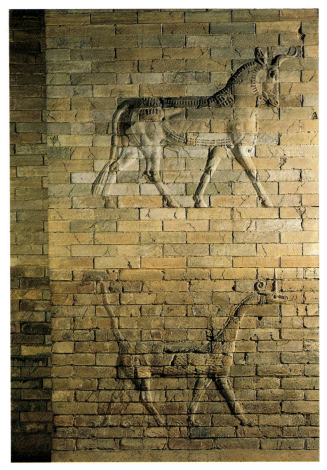

Fig. 12 Bull and dragon relief from the covering of the Ishtar Gate's facade, first building phase (Gallery 6 of the Museum)

clad in glazed, relief bricks. It is the Ishtar Gate whose smaller, northern part has been partially rebuilt in the Vorderasiatisches Museum *(fig. 9)*.

The reconstruction in the Museum, following the excavation findings as closely as possible, was carried out between 1929 and 1930. The measurement of the gateway door and both its flanking towers is based on its actual ground plan at Babylon. The height of the gateway, 14.75 meters, is an estimated height like that of the Processional Way based on considerations of proportion and practicality. The general design of the Museum's reconstruction of the building was adapted from representations of gateways found on gold plaques from a necklace discovered in a tomb in Babylon. The battlements were redesigned in a similar manner and supported by the fact that a number of bricks were found with appropriately stepped and glazed edges.

The new walls of the gateway, like the previous, were decorated with alternating rows of bulls and dragons assembled in the manner already discussed. The blue background was still to be found on the remains of the second building phase. The same can be said for the rosettes and the geometric bands. The quantity of blue brick fragments alone found during the excavation justifies the reconstruction of the entire facade in glazed bricks. In addition, the Ishtar Gate was the most important part of the building complex and for this reason distinguished itself from the Processional Way. For the Museum visitor, it is easy to see that the non-figural parts of the facade are imitation bricks. One should, however, also keep in mind that in the Museum reconstruction the animals stand with their feet on the same ground line, and in Babylon, because of the brick laying method, the animals around the corners stood one brick higher or lower.

One has to imagine a far larger gate behind the reconstructed gate in the Museum, which like the side walls, was simply too large to be rebuilt in the Museum. All walls of the gateway visible to the ancient Babylonians bore representations of animals symbolic of the gods and numbering at least 575 if we include those from the earlier building stages. Together with the lions of the Processional Way, the bulls and dragons of the gateway greeted the visitor to the capital of the Babylonian empire as he approached its gate. In addition, the animals were an ever present reminder to the population that the gods were omnipresent. This function was particularly important because the magnificent New Year Procession passed through the Ishtar Gate, another reason why the Gate was more impressively decorated than the other gateways.

On the other hand, when we examine the ground plan of the Processional Way and the Ishtar Gate, it is obvious

made a new filling of the entire area necessary. In the process the Processional Way was raised to its final height of over 15 meters. Simultaneously its walls were built up and decorated with the lion friezes and about 200 meters further, bastions were erected which created a northern boundary.

As the surrounding area was again filled, another part of the second building phase on the Ishtar Gate disappeared beneath the pavement. In the meantime, the glazed, flat brick technique had been developed further to the glazed relief bricks used for the lions along the Processional Way. In order to give the gate and the Processional Way a uniform appearance, Nebuchadnezzar quite naturally used the relief bricks for his new gate construction.

This last building representing the third building stage was

Fig. 13   Bull relief in flat-glaze technique from the covering of the Ishtar Gate's façade, second building phase (Gallery 6 of the Museum)

that they were very sophisticated defense structures where it was almost impossible for the enemy to find a weak spot. Before an enemy could even reach the only neuralgic point, the gateway, he would be turned away by the defense from the walls and the bastions.

That the troops of the Persian King, Kyros II (559−529 B.C.) succeeded in conquering the city in 539 B.C. is to be attributed to the altered political situation, not a weakness in the buildings. Whereas Nebuchadnezzar through his policy of conquest significantly expanded the empire and

became the central power in the Near East, its decline was pre-programmed under his successor, Awil-Marduk. In the following years, king succeeded king until 555 B.C. when Nabuna'id (−538 B.C.) ascended the throne. Not only had the empire been weakened by the Persians, but the system of domestic politics was totally inappropriate. Although the last king of Babylon erected buildings in the capital, his preference for the cult of the moon god, in the city of Harran, combined with his absence from the capital as well as his interference in the economy of the country, and his

Fig. 14a Fitting of the bricks with the reconstructed inscription of Nebuchadnezzar II on the Ishtar Gate in Berlin

pursuit of a policy which ran against the interests of the Babylonian priesthood who controled the economy led to his failure. There is no wonder, then, that the priesthood withdrew their support from their rightful king. They turned toward the new power in the Near East, Persia. In 539 B.C., two Persian armies penetrated Babylonia and on the 16th of Tashritu (September/October), the troops marched without resistance into Babylon. Babylonia became a Persian province. With time, the former capital lost its importance and even Alexander the Great's plan to make Babylon the capital of his world empire faltered with his early death in the city. The buildings were simply left to decay.

Almost 2500 years passed before archaeologists freed the remains of these marvelous buildings from the soil. Thanks to these archaeologists and many other friends of Near Eastern antiquities, visitors today may admire the skill of the Babylonian master builders.

THE FIRST AND SECOND CONSTRUCTION PHASES
(In Gallery 6 of the Museum)

Excavation findings at the Ishtar Gate yielded — as stated above — at least two different techniques of façade decoration in preserved state. The lower part of the edifice, which following the excavations was preserved to the greatest height, was lined with unglazed, relief bricks. Although we must assume that this technique of lining was employed only in the case of the façade of the gate, still the quite rough workmanship on the lower levels of the original is remarkable, since it stands in stark contrast to the uppermost preserved level of these unglazed animals, of which the row of bulls was later smoothed and covered with white plaster. During a short interval, it must have still been visible under the already colored glazed façade of the second stage.

Altogether 4 animals from this lower, uncolored part of the

gate construction have been reconstructed here, of which however only the exemplar to the lower left (behind glass) consists entirely of original fragments. The other three are plaster casts from the originals *(fig. 12)*.

Above the unglazed first construction level, remains of a further, in this case colored glazed lining were preserved. This mantel consisted of in some cases still well preserved representations of bulls which had been fashioned employing the technique of flat surface glazing. It was determined that these belonged to the lowest part of the second construction level of the Ishtar Gate. A reconstruction of some of these elements may be found along the longitudinal wall of this hall *(fig. 13, partially behind glass)*.

Three animals, bulls of the god Adad ideally reconstructed from unearthed fragments, can be seen here. We have dispensed with the row of dragons which stood above this frieze, however, since they may be seen in several other reconstructions in the exhibition. As a supplement to the animals, we have tried to show in the middle the original combination of the figures with the ornaments surrounding them done in the technique of flat surface glazing.

THE INSCRIPTION OF NEBUCHADNEZZAR II

The last great king of Babylonia recorded his building activity in inscriptions praising the gods, the well being of the city of Babylon and the immortality of his name. The most comprehensive of these inscriptions is the so-called "Great Stone Slab Inscription", today in London.

In the course of the excavation, numerous fragments with the remains of white cuneiform characters were found in the immediate vicinity of the gateway. They must have belonged to an inscription of King Nebuchadnezzar II's on the Ishtar Gate. Although the exact content of the inscription and its original position on the gateway are not known, a number of fragments were so well preserved that there can be no question as to the subject of the inscription, it concerned the building of the Ishtar Gate. Three segments from the inscription mentioned above have been included in the reconstruction to the left of the gate *(fig. 14a and b)*, and may be translated as follows:

Lines 1—23

"Nebuchadnezzar, King of Babylon, the pious prince appointed by the will of Marduk, the highest priestly prince, beloved of

Fig. 14b General view of the inscription of Nebuchadnezzar II

Nabu, of prudent deliberation, who has learnt to embrace wisdom, who fathomed Their (Marduk and Nabu) godly being and pays reverence to Their Majesty, the untiring Governor, who always has at heart the care of the cult of Esagila and Ezida and is constantly concerned with the well being of Babylon and Borsippa, the wise, the humble, the caretaker of Esagila and Ezida, the first born son of Nabopolassar, the King of Babylon, am I."

Lines 24—53

"Both gate entrances of the (city walls) Imgur-Ellil and Nemetti-Ellil following the filling of the street from Babylon had become increasingly lower. (Therefore,) I pulled down these gates and laid their foundations at the water table with asphalt and bricks and had them made of bricks with blue stone on which wonderful bulls and dragons were depicted. I covered their roofs by laying majestic cedars lengthwise over them. I fixed doors of cedar wood adorned with bronze at all the gate openings. I placed wild bulls and ferocious dragons in the gateways and thus adorned them with luxurious splendor so that Mankind might gaze on them in wonder."

Lines 54—60

"I let the temple of Esiskursiskur, the highest festival house of Marduk, the lord of the gods, a place of joy and jubilation for the major and minor deities, be built firm like a mountain in the precinct of Babylon of asphalt and fired bricks."

THE MODEL OF THE ISHTAR GATE AND THE PROCESSIONAL WAY

A model of the Ishtar Gate and part of the Processional Way are displayed in Gallery 9 of the Museum. The model shows the third and uppermost building phase *(fig. 15)*. The section of the Processional Way at the front of the model shows the various filling stages, each distinguished by a different color. It is also possible to see just how much higher than the surrounding area the Processional Way and the Ishtar Gate were.

The lion friezes along the walls of the Processional Way are shown as are the smaller gates that led from the sides to other parts of the building. The doors which originally

Fig. 15 View of the model of the Processional Way and Ishtar Gate, detail with the gate, the forecourt and the bastions

belonged to these gates and the Ishtar Gate itself have not been shown.

On the model, the division of the gateway into two parts aligned with the double fortification walls, the Imgur-Ellil and the Nemetti-Ellil, is also easily understood. Before it stands the newer wall erected by Nebuchadnezzar. Like the original, the walls are firmly anchored in the gateway and the city walls. The proportional height of the gateway over the entrance passage in the model does not correspond exactly with the reconstruction in the museum.

To the right and left behind the model of the gate, ground plans of the vaulted buildings in the south palace and the Ninmah Temple are partially visible.

Representations of palm columns with volute capitals and elaborate borders of flowers decorate the upper parts of the walls of the throne room. The use of varying shades of white, ochre and blue lend liveliness to the ornamentation.

The lions, rosette borders and portions of the lower palmette friezes on the facades, as well as the pair of volute and palmette borders to the left of the gate are original. To facilitate the assembly of the design, the Babylonian craftsmen coded the bricks (fig. 17). Using these marks, between 1899 and 1901 Walter Andrae succeeded in reconstructing the major part of the facade. Andrae's finding made the reconstruction of sections of the facade in the Museum possible.

THE FACADE OF THE THRONE ROOM

Two sections of the facade from the throne room of the southern palace of Babylon have been reconstructed on the narrow walls of Gallery 9 (see map of the Royal Palaces of Babylon).

The facade of the throne room situated south of the central and largest of the five palace courtyards was 56 meters wide. The massive wall foundations suggest walls of considerable height. The type of roofing used for this building is still not certain. Although Nebuchadnezzar frequently mentions cedar wood roofs in his inscriptions, (the beams would have to have had a diameter of at least 75 centimeters), no evidence of cedar beams were found during the excavations. On the other hand, it seems unlikely that a brick barrel vault spanned the ceiling, because the brick walls would not have been strong enough to support such a structure. Therefore, the height of the facade is not certain.

Therefore, the height of the walls has been determined by the height of the Museum gallery (fig. 16). Here, colored, glazed bricks cover the entire wall as they did on the Ishtar Gate. The lower part of the wall has been aligned with the Processional Way. It, too, is decorated with a frieze of lions who, in contrast to those on the Processional Way, hold their tails erect. Additional brick molds and at least one work model were, of course, necessary to make this variation possible.

From the right and the left, the lion friezes, which were perhaps arranged symmetrically, approached the entrance to the central and largest throne room. Because the throne room had three different entrances, the lion friezes were also interrupted once on each side.

Fig. 16 Reconstructed part of the Throne Room's facade from the southern palace of Nebuchadnezzar II in the Vorderasiatisches Museum

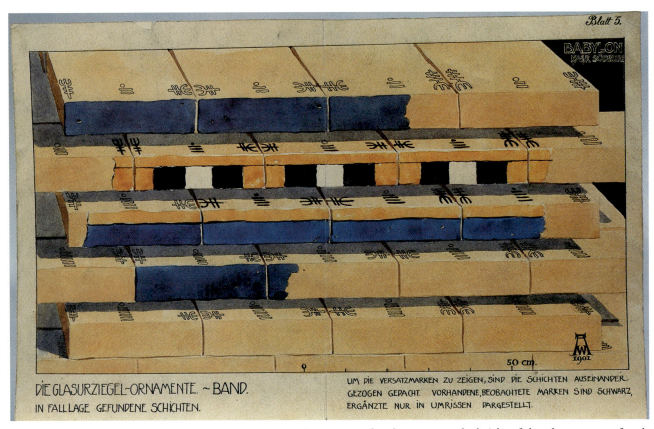

Blatt 5.

BABYLON
KASR SÜDBURG

DIE GLASURZIEGEL-ORNAMENTE. ~ BAND.
IN FALLLAGE GEFUNDENE SCHICHTEN.

UM DIE VERSATZMARKEN ZU ZEIGEN, SIND DIE SCHICHTEN AUSEINANDER
GEZOGEN GEDACHT. VORHANDENE, BEOBACHTETE MARKEN SIND SCHWARZ,
ERGÄNZTE NUR IN UMRISSEN DARGESTELLT.

50 cm.

Fig. 17   A watercolour by Walter Andrae showing the marking-system for placement on the bricks of the Throne Room facade

FURTHER BUILDINGS IN BABYLON

There are two reasons why we are relatively well informed about the appearance of Babylon in its heyday. In the first place, literary tradition played a major role. In the second, the excavators of the city pressed to the limits the then current scientific techniques and the possibilities afforded by local conditions. Examples of the results of this joint philological inquiry and archaeological fieldwork are to be found in Room 6 (Babylonian Hall) of our Museum.

THE CITY DESCRIPTION OF BABYLON

Part of the important literary traditions about Babylon are the accounts in the Old Testament about the time of the Babylonian exile of the Jews (2 Kgs. 24 and 25; 2 Chron. 36) as well as the still current story of the "Tower of Babylon" (Gen. 11). A further literary heritage is represented in the accounts of such ancient travellers as Herodotus (ca. 460 B.C.), Strabo, Diodorus and Q. Curtius Rufus (around the time of Christ and into the 1st century A.D.).

Today, however, the original texts, written in Babylonian cuneiform, are of much greater importance. We may include here both building and devotional inscriptions, as well as public and private legal texts, administrative documents, letters, religious literature, etc. A selection of these genres may be found in Room 6 of the exhibition (see case 15).

One of the most important witnesses is the so-called "City Description of Babylon," a series of five clay tablets. This series, written in the time before Nebuchadnezzar, describes the town in the form of a register. Besides the names and epithets of Babylon we find the seats of the gods in the main temple as well as an enumeration of temples and sanctuaries, town gates, walls, canals, streets and districts *(fig. 18a)*. 51 religious and cultic epithets alone are mentioned. Additionally, the list of epithets also contains references to the numerous cult festivals and the status of Babylon based on them:

"...
Babylon, the city of festivity, joy and dance;
Babylon, the city whose inhabitants celebrate constantly;
Babylon, the privileged city that frees the captive;
Babylon, the pure city;
Babylon, the city of goods and chattels;
Babylon, the bond of countries."

Following a list of the seats of gods, the fourth tablet contains the rank of the temples. First of all the sanctuaries of Marduk, namely Esagila and Etemenanki, are named. The fifth tablet of the series continues with the estrades of Marduk, the gates and walls, etc., to finally summarize *(fig. 18b)*:

"... *43 cult centers of the great gods of Babylon;*
55 estrades of Marduk; 2 surrounding walls; 3 rivers;
8 city gates; 24 streets of Babylon . . .
(Altogether:) 10 city (districts), whose fields (produce) abundance.

Fifth tablet: TIN.TIR, i.e. Babylon, entirely finished,
true to the wording of the tablets,
copies from Babylon, inscribed and collated,
tablet of Nabu-kin-ablim, the son of Ili-Marduk."

Excavations have been able to confirm the exactness of the Babylonian text. Leaving aside the unnamed royal palaces, eight temple complexes, the surrounding walls with four

Fig. 18 a Fragment of a clay tablet from the series with the "description of the city of Babylon", detail of the fourth tablet

Fig. 18 b Fragment, like Fig. 18a, fifth tablet, end of the text with a three-line signature of the entire work

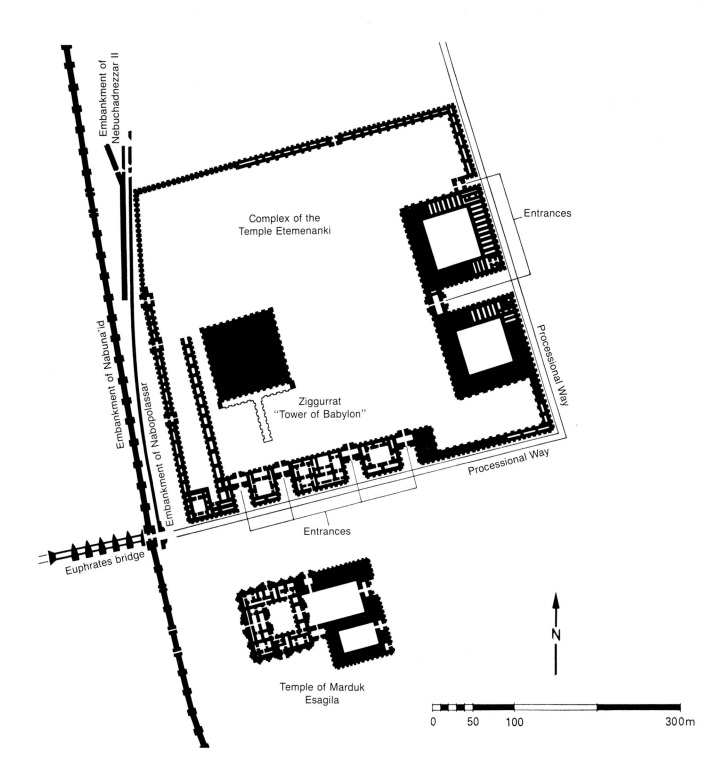

Fig. 19 Schematic ground plan of the Marduk sanctuary in the center of Babylon. Above: complex of the temple tower; below: the god's low temple. Condition at the beginning of the 6th century B.C.

gates as well as several streets have as of now been uncovered. This makes clear that Babylon was in a way the result of early city planning, which with an area of more than 16 km^2 seems only too natural. Both halves of the city had 4 gates each which were connected by main roads. One of these — Aj-ibur-shapu — has been presented in detail.

The districts, known by name, were grouped around the city center on the banks of the Euphrates. Here were situated the major sanctuaries of the city.

At the same time, a number of sanctuaries were to be found in the outer districts — quite comparable to modern cities.

THE MAJOR SANCTUARIES OF BABYLON

The temple tower Etemenanki

The most important building in the city was the double sanctuary of the national and city god Marduk in the center, whose holy symbols — the dragons — have already been described. With an extension of ca. 180 x 125 meters of the major temple at ground level (so-called "low temple"), Esagila, and ca. 460 x 410 meters of the temple tower complex Etemenanki, this was the most massive walled-in space of which Babylon of the 6th century B.C. could boast (cf. fig. 19).

It was already common in southern Mesopotamia in the 4th millennium B.C. to set off certain sanctuaries against their surroundings using terraced mounds. The development of such distantly visible temples was more or less completed already toward the end of the 3rd millennium B.C. A high terrace consisting of several levels came about, the so-called stepped tower — Babylonian "Ziqqurrat" — which was consistently crowned by a temple. The most famous example of this construction is the Ziggurrat of Ur, which remains today quite well preserved.

The construction history of the Ziggurrat of Babylon can only be deduced indirectly, however, since this building is established solely by historical accounts of it, beginning with inscriptions of Assyrian origin. It is thus known that King Sennacherib (705–681 B.C.) ordered the city together with its sanctuaries destroyed in the year 689. His successors Esarhaddon (681–669) and Assurbanipal (669–631/29 B.C.) dedicated themselves to the reconstruction of the sanctuaries. The best documented period is of course that of the regencies of Nabopolassar and Nebuchadnezzar; the building activity of this period was also best preserved.

The reason for this state of preservation is to be found in a new method of construction. Instead of the usual mud bricks which required constant restoration, the mantel surrounding the core of the tower was now laid with baked bricks. Nabopolassar states in his devotional inscription:

"Once . . . I had subdued Assyria at the behest of (the gods) Nabu and Marduk, who love my kingship, . . . Marduk, my Lord, ordered me to secure the foundation of Etemenanki, the Ziggurrat of Babylon which before my time had gone into disrepair, on the bottom of the construction pit (literally: breast of the netherworld) and to let its summit vie with the heavens . . .

I made and had made (common mud) bricks, had baked bricks produced, countless as rain from the heavens. Like a massive flood did I have mortar and asphalt brought via the Arakhtu (= Euphrates) . . .

Before Marduk, my Lord, did I lower my neck . . . and carry bricks and mud on my head . . . and I let Nebuchadnezzar, the first-born, the eldest, the favorite of my heart, carry together with my people mud, wines, oil and herbs."

Nabopolassar boasted, certainly with good cause, of his improvements of earlier constructions; however, he was not to experience himself the completion of his plans. It fell to his "first-born, the favorite one of his heart," Nebuchadnezzar, to finish the massive work. He then also reported among other things in his inscription:

"Etemenanki, the Ziggurrat of Babylon, whose site Nabopolassar, the king of Babylon, my father and begetter . . . cleansed, and whose foundation he erected on the bottom of the construction pit, whose four walls he erected roundabout with asphalt and baked bricks to a height of 30 cubits — its summit (however) he did not elevate. I went about to elevate Etemenanki, to let its summit vie with the heavens, . . .

A (pure) high temple, a (well guarded) cella as in earlier days I erected artfully for Marduk, my Lord, on its superstructure."

The sections of the inscription show that the edifice was meant to be founded as if "for eternity." Immeasurable quantities of materials, labor, tools and provisions must have been used for the completion of this task. The mentioned mantel of bricks alone, whose thickness at the lowest building level measured 18 meters, required, according to calculations of the excavator H. J. Schmid, from 10 to 14 million bricks — Nabopolassar thus knew exactly what he was describing.

Despite the durable materials, the tower was to enjoy no long existence. Already during the reign of Xerxes (486–465 B.C.), the temples of the city were, following rebellions in Babylonia, looted, the walls razed, the statue of Marduk destroyed; the Euphrates was even diverted through the city quarters. During his visit to Babylon in the middle of the 5th century B.C., Herodotus will have met with no more than a sanctuary in severe disrepair.

The plan of Alexander the Great to fully restore the tower, finally, led unfortunately to its demise. Due to Alexander's untimely death, only the removal of the debris of the old building was achieved. Remains of this debris were found in excavations in the northeast section of the city, in the vicinity of the later Greek theater. Brick thieves of later centuries contributed to the further destruction of the ruins.

R. Koldewey in 1913 and H. J. Schmid in 1962 were able to examine the building core of the tower and the negative impression of the removed building mantel, which was still preserved in the ground. In its place extended a trench filled with ground-water, which can still be seen today. (fig. 19 and 20) Fortunately for the investigation, the brick thieves had often left the outermost edges of the walls intact, so that here the dimensions of the tower could be established.

Additional information was provided by a cuneiform document discovered in the 19th century, now in the collections of the Louvre, the so-called "Esagila-Tablet." The text seems to contain a kind of mathematical exercise in the form of a listing of dimensions. Beyond the building description of the temple Esagila, the objects of consideration are the different building levels of the temple tower Etemenanki. Considered together with the excavation finds and the other inscriptions, the text offers the possibility to reconstruct the appearance of the famous "Tower of Babylon" in its essential aspects.

Our current understanding may accordingly be summarized as follows (cf. the model of the sanctuary in Room 6 of the exhibition and fig. 21):

In the middle of the city of Babylon, on the east bank of the Euphrates, lay — surrounded by a massive enclosing wall — the stepped tower 'E-temen-an-ki,' "the house of the foundation of heaven and earth." Out of a substructure of 91,48 x 91,66 meters, the height of which was in the original given as 30 cubits, that is, about 15 meters, the tower developed in all together five more levels, one smaller than the other. On its "head" stood the high temple of Marduk. The total elevation of the building would have corresponded to the measurements of its base. That is to say, the tower rose to the — for its time — enormous height of ca. 90 meters.

Access to the upper levels was gained over three flights of stairs whose remains could still be traced. Two of these rose from the corners of the southern wall. The direct access, which was certainly of cultic importance, resulted from a stairway leading into the building from the south. Its outline with a length of 50 meters and a width of 10 meters is visible to this day (fig. 20). Unfortunately, it has not been finally determined what course the stairs took above the first level. So the model shown here is just one proposal for a reconstruction. This should not lessen, however, the impression one has today concerning the total effect of the structure.

In the high temple itself, there were, beyond the Holy of Holies of Marduk, further rooms of worship for his divine son, the god of writing, Nabu, and his consort Tashmetu.

The lord of wisdom, Ea, was, moreover, worshiped here, as well as the gods Anu, Nusku and Enlil.

As a chosen site and as a central place in communal life, the temple district Etemenanki was a witness of the times whose dimensions still demand of us admiration today. It was a place which played a central role in the beliefs of the Babylonians. The gods of the country came here for the New Year's festival (cf. the final chapter of this brochure), the riches of the powerful priesthood of Marduk were gathered here. This was the central place of the famous Babylonian scholarship, the refuge of the sciences and of writing—that cultural achievement of Mesopotamia from which our modern tradition of writing emerged.

The low temple Esagila

Although up to now only the temple tower has been discussed, we cannot separate it from the nearby low temple, i. e., the temple complex of Marduk erected at ground-level. Both of these Mesopotamian architectural components formed one unit, so that the low temple Esagila, "the House of the Headraising," is neither in its construction nor in its content to be separated from Etemenanki. Their cultic connection was established by the procession street Aj-ibur-shapu running between them, which allowed equal access to both sanctuaries.

The ruins of Esagila, which lay in places under 20 meters high rubbish, allowed in long stretches merely the digging of tunnels with shafts for lighting or a relatively constricted surface excavation. Just the same, the entire expanse of the ancient temple could be established in this manner, according to which a division of the structure into a central building with an addition extending to the front became evident.

The division of its façade into niches corresponded to that of the temple tower; this was only extended at the doors to form coupled towers. The walls were preserved to a height of 10 meters in places and were in relatively good condition. The central part to the west possessed a large inner courtyard from which the surrounding wings of the building could be entered. These were designed as complex rooms

Fig. 20 Areal view of the present day condition of the temple tower's ruins from Babylon

and represented chapel-like sanctuaries, which were dedicated to the gods of the Babylonian pantheon. The cellae of several deities were identified with some certainty, among them those of Ea, Nabu, Tashmetu and the consort of Marduk, the goddess Sarpanitu. The Holy of Holies, the cella of Marduk himself, was, however, not to be found.

Even though our portrait seems thus reduced to impressive edifices, it is worth stressing that the real wealth of a Babylonian temple laid in its position within the ancient society. The position of the sanctuary was constituted by more than just privileges such as exemption from taxes, land ownership and the use of often extensive personnel, who worked in temple-owned workshops or who as contractors conducted business in trade, real estate and finance. Above all, the numerous festivals, mostly lasting several days, reflecting the events of life in mythological-ritual form, created that level of "Sitz im Leben" — nowadays difficult to understand — which in particular the high temple of the Babylonian empire once enjoyed.

Esagila can as it were be seen as the temple in the middle of city life. Etemenanki, on the other hand, seems to have represented that component of the same idea which strove toward the heavens. Both elements were inseparable and mutually conditioning and should thus be understood independent of the still current tradition of the "Tower of Babylon."

Fig. 21 Model of the Marduk sanctuary in Babylon. Detail with the reconstruction of the temple tower Etemenanki

Fig. 22 The lower sections of the temple tower's core in Babylon after the excavations of 1962

THE BABYLONIAN NEW YEAR FESTIVAL

The street, Aj-ibur-shapu, and the gate, Ishtar-sakipat-tebisha, today known as the Processional Way and the Ishtar Gate of Babylon, thanks to their reconstruction in the Museum are now famous worldwide. Although we have discussed the Gate and the Processional Way in detail, we have said little about the function of the buildings which was far more than a citadel. To understand these buildings we must turn to the building inscriptions of the Babylonian kings.

The Ishtar Gate and the Processional Way were more important than the other city gates and streets because they acted as the background for the New Year procession. Even the decoration of the walls, animals sacred to the gods, is a reference to the role these buildings played in this important religious festival. There is no evidence that any of the other city gates were decorated in a similar manner. To understand the historical and religious significance of the Ishtar Gate and the Processional Way, it is necessary to have an idea of the Babylonian New Year Festival.

Most of us follow the Julian Calendar and celebrate the New Year on January 1 shortly after the winter equinox. It may come as a surprise that until 1712 the New Year was celebrated on March 26 in England. Until 1556 the New Year began for the French on Easter, and only since 1776 in Germany has the New Year been celebrated on the first of January. Even today in Islamic countries the New Year begins at different times. In these countries the Islamic calendar is not based on the solar year but on the shorter lunar year.

In the ancient Near East, since the third millennium B.C., the year was divided into months. Because the phases of the moon determined the calendar, a difference quite naturally developed between the lunar year and the actual time the earth needed to orbit the sun. This difference was particularly obvious when one observed the course of nature. Beginning around the end of the third millennium, attempts had been made to correct the difference with "leaping". Leaping necessitated an occasional "leap month" which was added by royal decree when the difference between the calendar and the occurrence of natural events became too pronounced.

So, in fact, the course of the year followed natural conditions like the spring floods and the ripening of crops. In Babylonia the New Year started in the spring when the earth returned to life around the time of the spring equinox. It varied accordingly if a "leap month" had been added. Each year was divided into 12 months. The sixth and the twelfth month were possible "leap months" which would then be counted twice:

1. Nisannu (March/April)
2. Aiaru (April/May)
3. Simanu (May/June)
4. Du'uzu (June/July)
5. Abu (July/August)
6. Ululu (August/September)
7. Tashritu (September/October)
8. Arahsamna (October/November)
9. Kislimu (November/December) our New Year today
10. Tebetu (December/January)
11. Sabatu (January/February)
12. Addaru (February/March)

The number of days in a month were 29 or 30, alternately. Other than being associated with a particular phase of the moon, they had no special names. So, in Babylonia the year began with the first of Nisannu and ended with the 30th of Addaru.

We know that the Akitu Festival, a multi-day festival for major temples, was already celebrated in Babylonia in the second half of the third millennium where a number of buildings for its celebration are documented. Early on the Akitu Festival was combined with the New Year Festival, Zagmukku, celebrated at the beginning of Nisannu. In this way, the Babylonian New Year Festival reached its level of importance and compass.

The New Year Festival was the ritual beginning of the agricultural year and was meant to guarantee divine blessings for the soil's fertility as well as the prosperity of the state. Therefore, the festival which was celebrated in honor of the great state god, Marduk, with the king playing the pivotal role, was considered indispensable to the maintenance of the religion and the state. Each year anew, the king must court the goodwill of His Lord, Marduk, and beg for Marduk's mercy in the name of Babylonia. The official documents, of course, do not tell us if an agreement of interests with the powerful Babylonian priesthood stood in the background.

From the first to the 11th of Nisannu, the city of Babylon and with it the entire country celebrated this great festival.

The main part of the festival took place in the Esagila temple and the Etemenanki temple (see map of Babylon, endpaper). The festive procession of the gods to the New Year Festival temple began on the 9th of Nisannu and ended on the 11th of Nisannu with the return of the statues of the gods to their city.

The contemporary inscriptions and cultic and mythological texts tell us a great deal about Babylon's most important festival.

Unfortunately, however, they do not give us enough information to follow its entire course. The most comprehensive text describing the ritual for the New Year Festival in Babylon, stops at the 5th of Nisannu. In addition, a number of gaps in the text complicate its understanding. Another text from Uruk in southern Mesopotamia which could supplement the text is, however, datable to the third century B.C. Other texts with details about the New Year Festival have been found in Assur, Nineveh and Harran. Because of the numerous gaps in these texts and their varied dates reconstruction of the New Year Festival is not easy. One cannot be certain that rituals held in Babylon were the same elsewhere and in some cases it is not even clear if they refer to the New Year Festival. On the other hand, it is important to recognize that this festival had been celebrated for hundreds of years and a certain continuity can be taken for granted. Although the subject of the New Year Festival in religious disputes at the beginning of this century, in more recent times, it has received little attention.

Only the discovery of new inscriptions can offer a final interpretation of the New Year Festival. Although Iraq is again excavating extensively in the area, there is of course no assurance that such inscriptions will be found.

Based on this information gathered from various sources, the New Year Festival was probably celebrated in the manner which will now be described.

The **first of Nisannu** marked the beginning of the festival. The following days were spent making preparations for the climax of the festival that took place in the Esagila, the main temple of Marduk (Bel). The protocol for the first day of the celebration has not been preserved. The ritual records the following points for the second day:

"*On the* **second day** *of the month of Nisannu, two hours (before the end of) the night, the sheshgallu priest (high priest) rises and washes himself with river water. He enters into the presence of Bel (the statue of Marduk in the inner sanctuary) and spreads (?) out a cloth of linen. He wakes before Bel (?) (him and) recites the following prayer:*

'*O Lord, who has no equal in his anger,*
O Lord, Gracious King, Lord of the Lands,
Who makes the great gods friendly,
O Lord, who fells the mighty with his glance.
O Lord, . . . the kings, light of mankind, who divides the portions,
O Lord, your dwelling is Babylon, Borsippa your tiara,
The broad heaven is the totality of your body.
O Lord, with your eyes you see all things,
(With) your oracles you verify the oracles (of other gods),
(With) your glance you hand down the law.
With your arms (?) you chain (?) the mighty,
Your . . . you grasp with your hands,
With your glance you grant them mercy.

You show them light, (and) they speak of your strength,
Lord of the Lands, light of the Igigu deities, who speak of you in a friendly manner,
Who is there that does not speak of your strength,
Who does not proclaim your glory, does not glorify your sovereignty?
Lord of the Lands, who dwells in the Euddul temple, who grasps the hand of the fallen,
Grant your city Babylon mercy!
To Esagila, your house, turn your face!!
For the Babylonians, the privileged citizens, cause liberty!'"

The prayer closes with the statement that the prayer is secret and only the sheshgallu priest may recite this prayer to Marduk. Up to this point, the sheshgallu priest was alone in the inner sanctum. He turns now to the door and opens it. Priests of varying ranks, members of the erib biti (those admitted to all temple parts), lamentation priests and singers waiting before the door enter to perform their daily rituals before Marduk and his divine spouse, Sarpanitu. The entrance of the priests to the inner sanctum is followed by another prayer, at which point the text breaks off leaving us uninformed about the end of the second day.

The **third day** begins as the second with the ritual washing by the high priest and the prayer followed by the arrival of the other priests. Three hours after sunrise, a metal worker receives the order to make a pair of statuettes out of precious stones and gold given to him from Marduk's treasure. In addition, a wood worker and a goldsmith were also commissioned to assist in the work. The date for the delivery of the finished parts of the statuettes is set from the third to the sixth of Nisannu and a detailed description is made for the comissioned statuettes. Arrangements are also made that the statues will be honored with offering until the sixth day, the day that the god Nabu arrives. Then the statuettes are to be decapitated and burned.

The **fourth day** of Nisannu begins already three and a half hours before sunrise as the high priest performs the usual rituals. On this day he not only recites the prayer to Marduk, but an additional one to Sarpanitu. Only after he has invoked the constellation of the ram (Aries) (it is still night) in the courtyard and blessed the sanctuary, are the other priests permitted to enter and get on with their tasks.

On the evening of the fourth of Nisannu, the high priest must fulfill a particularly important task. He approaches the image of the god and recites "from beginning to end (!)", the Epic of Creation, Enuma Elish. The beginning of the epic reads:

"*Once when the heaven on high had not been named,*
The earth below bore no name,
As Apsu, the primordial, their begetter,
Mummu (and) Tiamat, she who bore them all,

Its waters mixed as one,
The shrubs were not connected to one another,
The marsh was not to be seen,
As the gods did not exist, no one
had named them, their destinies undetermined,
Then the gods were created in their midst . . ."

The epic goes on to describe how the generations of gods came into being and how a rift developed between the old gods, Apsu, Mummu and Tiamat, and the newly created gods, Anu and Ea. Apsu is killed by Ea and Mummu is raped. As the son of Ea and his wife, Damkina, the child god, Marduk, is born. Tiamat decides to seek vengeance for the death of Apsu and creates furious dragons, dogs and composite beings to help her. As a result, the major gods are seized with fear and even Ea, whose wit never fails him, is downcast. He suggests that his son, Marduk, be commissioned to fight Tiamat. Marduk is ready to accept the challenge under one condition, he wants to be lord of all the gods! The gods, helpless, are forced to accept his condition and during a euphoric festival, they confer the rule of the gods on Marduk. Marduk goes then to fight Tiamat and wins. He creates the sky and the earth from her body and sets the sun, moon and the stars in the sky and on the earth creates the plants and the animals. As his crowning achievement, he creates mankind from the blood of Tiamat's lover. Man is supposed to take over the work of the gods. The epic closes with a hymn to Marduk and the naming of his fifty sacred names.

On the **fifth of Nisannu**, the sheshgallu priest arises four hours before sunrise, says his prayers before Marduk and Sarpanitu and admits the priests to the sanctuary. Two hours after sunrise, following the morning sacrifice to Marduk and Sarpanitu, an exorcist purifies the temple. To prevent contamination, the high priest is forbidden to be present during this ceremony.

In the course of the ritual cleansing, a remarkable rite is enacted. The sword bearer is called upon to cut off the head of a ram. The exorcist, while reciting purification incantations, must sweep the shrine of Nabu with the carcass of the ram. When this is finished, the sword bearer and the exorcist take the ram's carcass and head and throw them into the river. From the fifth to the twelfth of Nisannu, both men must remain outside the city on the plain and may only reenter Babylon once Nabu has left. This particular ceremony reminds one clearly of the scapegoat found in the Jewish and Hittite religions.

In the temple, craftsmen now cover the chapel of Nabu with a "golden sky". After the high priest has offered a sacrifice to Marduk and spoken a prayer, the offering table is removed from the Marduk's chapel and taken to Nabu's chapel to await the following day.

What now follows is perhaps the most curious part of the entire New Year Festival. The king is led into the temple by the priests where he remains standing alone before the chapel of Marduk. The sheshgallu priest appears and takes the king's royal insignia and brings them to Marduk. When the priest returns, he slaps the king, pulls his ears and requires that he prostrate himself before Marduk and recite a prayer of repentance. After this, the king is granted absolution on behalf of Marduk:

"Have no fear . . .
for Marduk has spoken . . .
Marduk will listen to your prayer . . .
He will increase your rule . . .
He will exalt your kingship . . . etc."

The king is now given back his royal regalia. Once again, the king is slapped and pulled on the ears until he sheds tears. When the king sheds tears it is considered a good omen and only now will Marduk be well disposed. It is not clear if the king plays the role of the penitent for the whole land in this ceremony.

On the same evening another sacrifice is made by the high priest in which a white bull plays a role. At this point the text is broken away.

In order to reconstruct as much as possible of the rest of the Festival, other sources have been drawn upon with a certain amount of caution as well as the version of the festival celebrated in Uruk.

In any case, on the **sixth of Nisannu**, the god Nabu arrived from Borsippa embodied by his statue. Nabu lived in Babylon's sister-city and was considered the son of Marduk and Sarpanitu. He was one of the most important gods and without his presence, the festival could not begin. Nabu was the god of writing and the patron god of scribes and therefore possessed special insight into the destiny of the world. He was the author of the tablets of destiny mentioned in the Epic of Creation which he temporarily kept in his temple. The possession of these tablets guaranteed rulership of the entire world.

For Nabu's visit to Babylon, a street similar to the Procession Way was built. It ran from his temple in Borsippa to the Borsippa canal which connected the city to Babylon. The statue of Nabu was probably transported to the canal on a richly decorated wagon with the procession making many stops along the way. The statue was then carried by boat to Babylon where it arrived on the sixth day of the festival. The Ritual says that a special chapel was built for Nabu in the temple of Marduk. Upon Nabu's arrival, the statuettes that had been ordered on the third day of Nisannu were destroyed.

In addition to Nabu, many other gods took part in the festival as statues. In another text we read:

"All the gods, the gods of Borsippa, Kuta, Kish and the gods of all the cult centers, in order 'to take the hand' of the great lord Marduk, come to Babylon and go with him to the festival temple. On the sixth day at sunrise, Anu and Enlil come to Babylon from Uruk and Nippur, in order to 'take the hand' of the Lord and go with him in procession to the house of prayer. Like them, all great gods also come to Babylon. All the gods who go with Marduk to the house of prayer, it is like a king whose army has assembled."

These gods, much like Nabu, were probably accommodated in special chapels in the Marduk Temple. Inscriptions as well as the excavation results show that numerous chapels once stood there.

In the days following the sixth of Nisannu, extensive rituals were performed whose course and location are not exactly clear. One of the most important was the determination of fate which was enacted by Marduk on the **eighth and ninth day**. This was connected with a procession of Marduk and Nabu to the parak shimati (high seat of destinies) of the ub-shukkinakku (assembly of gods) where the assembled gods paid homage to Marduk. It is probably during this meeting that oracles determined the fate of the country and its inhabitants, including the king.

The assembly room may have been situated in an annex of the Esagila sanctuary and the high seat in its courtyard. This part of the temple has never been completely excavated. On the occasion of this ceremony, a number of sacrifices and prayers were offered and a huge banquet was held which probably imitated the assembly of gods in the Epic of Creation.

The actual start of the procession, however, was the act of taking the hand of the god Marduk. The king symbolically took the hand of Marduk and bade him rise. With this began the procession of the gods from the city to the Akitu festival temple outside the city. Thus far, the site of the Akitu temple has not been discovered.

The course of the Processional Way shows that the Akitu temple must have been situated north of the inner city and in the vicinity of a river or canal because at least part of the procession took place on boats. According to preserved inscriptions, the temple seems to have been very simple.

Without doubt, the procession to Akitu temple must have been magnificent. The gods, led by Marduk, proceeded in their richly decorated thrones, followed by priests, praying and swinging thuribels and perhaps to the accompaniment of music. It is not difficult to imagine the citizens of Babylon and their guests lining the streets. Although the written sources do not tell us the route taken by the procession, the city could only have been left to the north. Whether the procession left the city through the Ishtar Gate and then proceeded on the canal to the festival temple, or, if the gods were pulled up the Euphrates to the canal on boats is not known. The way from the canal mooring to the festival temple was lined with trees forming a wooded glen, perhaps to emphasize the connection to nature.

Although we know little about the course of events in the festival temple, we do know, for instance, that the king offered numerous gifts to the gods.

On **the eleventh day**, the gods in festive procession returned by land to the city. It is specifically for this purpose that the Processional Way and the Ishtar Gate were so splendidly adorned. The population was permitted to participate in this part of the festival and it must have made a very lively picture. At the festival temple, a banquet had been provided and it was now time for Marduk to return to his city. With Marduk at its head, the procession of the gods, certainly accompanied by the king and followed by the masses headed toward Babylon. Marduk then proceeded through the Etemenanki sanctuary to the inner city and his temple. Nabu and the other gods returned to their own temples on the following days.

With this the largest and most important festival of the Babylonians came to a close and the year might take its course.

48 pages with 16 color- and 12 black-and-white-photographs

Photograph credits: Jürgen Liepe, Vorderasiatisches Museum,
G. Gerster, H. Schmid

Translation: Biri Fay and Robert K. Englund

Front cover: View of Gallery 9 in the Vorderasiatisches Museum
with the reconstruction of the Ishtar Gate and the facade of the
Throne Room from Babylon (6th century B.C.)

Endpapers: Detail of the model of the Processional Way and of
the Ishtar Gate from Babylon. Map of the Royal Palaces of
Babylon. Map of Babylon around 600 B.C.

Frontispiece: Reconstruction of the Ishtar Gate, frontal view

Back cover: Detail from one of the reconstructed Throne Room
facades from Babylon in the Vorderasiatisches Museum

© 1992 Staatliche Museen zu Berlin — Preußischer Kulturbesitz
Verlag Philipp von Zabern, Mainz on the Rhine

ISBN 3-8053-1333-0
ISBN 3-8053-1307-1 (Edition of Museum)
Layout: Lothar Bache
Type: Typo-Service Mainz
Lithography: SWS Repro GmbH, Wiesbaden
Paper: Papierfabrik Scheufelen, Lenningen
Printed in Germany/Imprimé en Allemagne
Manufactured by Verlag Philipp von Zabern
Printed on fade resistant and archival quality paper (PH 7 neutral)

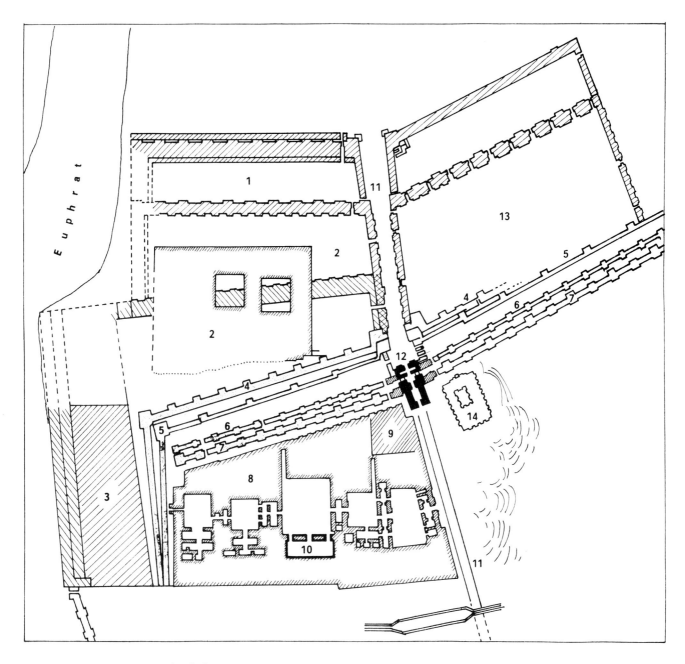

Map of the Royal Palaces of Babylon

1 Northern palace
2 Main palace
3 Outwork on the river
4 Younger Moat wall of Nebuchadnezzar II
5 Older Moat wall of Nebuchadnezzar II
6 City wall Nemetti-Ellil
7 City wall Imgur-Ellil

8 Southern palace ("City-Palace")
9 Vaulted building ("Hanging Gardens"?)
10 Throne Room of Nebuchadnezzar II
11 Processional Way
12 Ishtar Gate
13 So-called Eastern Outwork
14 Temple of Ninmah

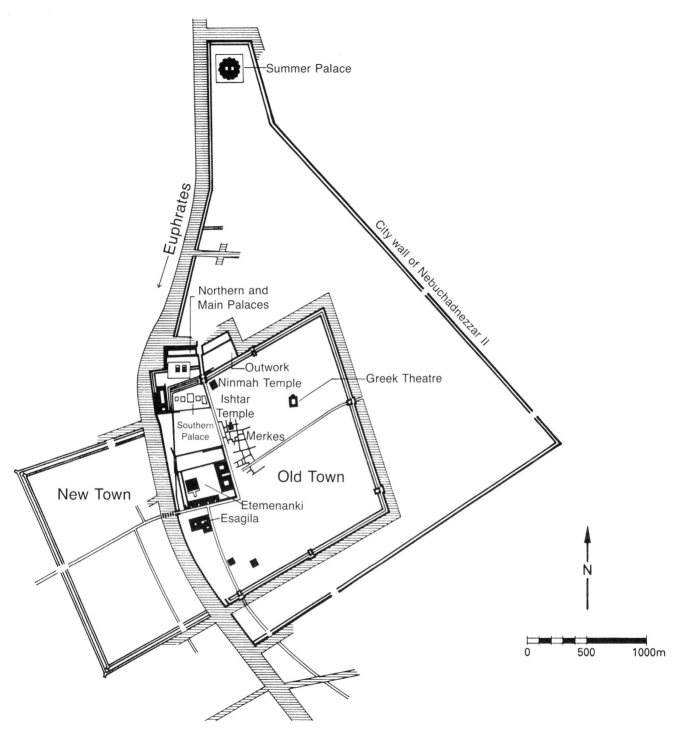

Map of Babylon around 600 B.C.